The Art of Writing a Eulogy

By

Dr. Rick Gillespie-Mobley

To My Wife Toby Lynne Gillespie-Mobley Who

Supports Me Constantly

To Samantha, Anita, Keon & Sharon For

Enriching Me

To My Mom Clarien Dixon For Believing In Me

To The Covenant Partners of New Life At Calvary

Who Pray For Me

To God For The Gifts He Gives To Me To Pass To

Others

Table of Contents

Meet The Author

Rick Gillespie-Mobley has been a pastor since 1983. The most appreciated part of his ministry through the years has been his gift to preach eulogies in such a way that even total strangers at the services have asked if he would preach their funeral. After one eulogy, a stranger came up to him after the service and said, "We came in with heavy and sad hearts, but you have truly lifted our spirits. Thank you."

Rick believes that everyone can learn to write good eulogies that minister to the lives of those who are present. He shares with you the steps he takes in order to craft eulogies in such a way, that people truly feel blessed. In doing the anatomy of a eulogy, Rick allows you to understand both the how and the why of putting together an effective eulogy. You can use your eulogy to be a celebration of a person's life while at the same time pointing the audience in the direction of God. The audience will appreciate your ministry in an even greater way than before.

Rick was married on August 30, 1980 to his bride Toby. They have served together as co-pastors for nearly 30 years. In addition to their adult children Samantha, Anita, Keon, and Sharon, they have served as foster parents for 20 years. Rick is a graduate of Hornell Senior High School in Hornell, NY, Hamilton College B.A. in Clinton, NY, Gordon Conwel Theological Seminary M. Div. in S. Hamilton, Ma, Trinity Bible College & Seminary D. Min in Newburgh , In and Boston University School of Law J.D.

Rick has served with his wife Toby as co-pastors of Roxbury Presbyterian Church in Boston, Ma, Glenville New Life Community Church in Cleveland, Oh, New Life Fellowship in Cleveland, OH, Calvary Presbyterian Church in Cleveland, OH. They now serve together on a pastoral team with Kellie Sullivan and Willie Nieves at New Life At Calvary in Cleveland, OH. Rick and Toby were both ordained in the Presbyterian Church of the United States Of America, but have since transferred their membership to A Covenant Order of Evangelical Presbyterian (ECO). Rick was admitted to practice law in both Massachusetts and Ohio.

Introduction-What's A Eulogy

Every life is a gift from God that tells a story. Each year that is lived is a chapter or subchapter of a person's life. Just as each book has a beginning and an end, each life has its beginning and its end. At the end of each life there is a funeral, a memorial service, a time of remembrance, a home-going service or something similar to acknowledge the life and death of a person.

A eulogy is an opportunity to celebrate the life of a person and to lift the hearts of those who have been left behind. Whereas I use the term eulogy, others may call it a meditation, a sermon, a speech or a short talk. The word being used does not really matter, because the purpose is still the same. I have been to services in which very little is said at all of the deceased person, and instead a sermon is preached in order to prepare others for the reality of death. The sermon begins with, "John

Doe has preached his life and there is nothing more that I can say about him, but I do want to tell you this”.. . and off the sermon goes. We can do better than that, especially for our brothers and sisters in Christ.

The reason we preach sermons on Abraham, Sarah, Lot, Moses, David, Solomon, Peter, Judas, Paul, Mary, John and many other characters in the Bible is that we believe their lives are still speaking to us even today. In reality, the lives of those Biblical characters are no different than the lives of people today. They were flesh and bones imperfect human beings whom God called to be in a relationship to him. The stories of their lives continue to speak to us, even though they died centuries ago. The stories of their lives are actually mini-eulogies recorded in the Scriptures for our spiritual development.

The goal of this book is to equip you with a strategy on writing a good eulogy that can both comfort the hearts of the audience, while showing how God is at work in the life of the person who has died. This is especially true in the life of the believer. Jesus can be preached from that person's life, just as well as He can be preached from the life of Joseph or Mary Magdalene. Every believer's life is a testimony of God's grace and mercy.

To write and speak a good eulogy is going to require some work on your part. You will need to actively engage the participation of others in order to be the most effective. There may be times when you cannot follow all the steps that are listed, but even following some, will make your eulogy more effective. I have attempted to make this book as practical as possible. I will do an anatomy of a eulogy to take you along in the process so that you can understand why certain things are done in the manner in which they are done. The good news is that an ordinary person can write a great eulogy. If you write sermons already, you have a jump on those who have not.

The Interviewing Process

A good eulogy requires some investigative reporting. Although we may think of the book of Luke as the gospel of Jesus Christ, it could also be considered as eulogy for Jesus Christ because it tells of his life and his death. But in order for Luke to put his eulogy together he wrote the following:

> [1] Many have undertaken to draw up an account of the things that have been fulfilled among us, [2] just as they were handed down to us by those who from the first were eyewitnesses and servants of the word. [3] With this in mind, since I myself have carefully investigated everything from the beginning, I too decided to write an orderly account for you, most excellent Theophilus, [4] so that you may know the certainty of the things you have been taught. **Luke 1:1-4 (TNIV)**

Luke began by interviewing people who had a firsthand knowledge of Jesus and finding out from them what exactly took place. He actually went out to talk with people who had been with Jesus, heard what he said, and saw what he did. He then gathered his notes and put everything in an orderly account so that others could make sense of it all.

The first step in preparing a good eulogy is to gather a group of people together who knew the deceased and begin to interview them with questions about the decease. You may interview parents, children, spouses, siblings, relatives, friends, neighbors, and co-workers. The number of people available to you may be as little as one or as many as ten. Ask the family members to meet with you for about a ½ hour to an hour to help you with the eulogy.

Sometimes a face to face meeting is not possible, but even a phone conversation is better than no interviewing at all. You won't be able to get as much nonverbal communication about the deceased as you would if you were physically present. With today's technology, you can do better than the phone with video communication.

It is important for you to begin the meeting by saying, "I will be doing the eulogy (meditation or whatever you may call it) and I need your help to make it the best eulogy possible. I want to help those present at the service to get a glimpse into the life of _______________, and you are the best source for me to make it happen. I won't be using everything you say, but I do need your help. I'm going to ask you some questions and I want you to give me the first thing that comes to your mind. Remember there is no right or wrong answers."

Some families will provide you with more information than you can possibly use, and other families will all seem to have just drawn blank responses. Just give the people time to answer questions and to share their stories. Part of preparing the eulogy is listening to how others speak about the deceased. You can learn a lot from the dynamics that take place in the meeting.

Make sure you have your pen and paper ready or a recording device so as to remember what is shared. Get permission before using the recording device or let them know you are only using the recording devise to take notes and that it will not be shared with anyone else. Begin the process by asking the group for some one word descriptions that come to mind about the person. You can get them started by making suggestions such as “funny”, “serious”, “quiet”, or “loud.” Let the group continue to offer words until they run out of descriptions.

You will want to gather some historical background on the person to assist you later in the preparation of your eulogy. This will help provide you with various alternatives on how to begin your eulogy. Here is information you should seek to gather:

- When was the person born?
  - Where was the person born?
  - Who were the person’s parents?
  - Where did the person grow up?

- How many brothers and sisters did the person have?
- Where was the person's order in the line of brothers and sisters?
- Was the person married- if so when and how long?
- Did the person have children-if so and how many?

You want to get stories from the people that you are interviewing so that you can interweave some of them into a larger story of the person's life. Here are some additional questions to present. Whether or not you ask some of the questions will depend upon the person who has died and who you are able to interview?

- What was the person like as a child?
- What activities did the person participate in school?
- Where did the person attend school?

- What were the favorite things the person liked to do as a child?
- What was the person like as a brother or sister?
- What was the person's favorite food?
- What were the person's hobbies?

You can get a better picture of the person by asking questions that will allow the person sharing the stories to share their emotions about the person. It's good to ask these questions in terms of the person's relationship to the deceased for example, as a father, son, daughter, mother, grandparent, grandchild, friend etc.

- What's a special moment you shared with the person that meant a lot to you?
- What was a gift the person received that meant a lot to him/her?
- What was a gift that you received from the person that meant a lot to you and why?
- What holiday did the person enjoy the most?

- What was a funny moment you shared with the person?
- What will you miss the most about the person being gone?

If the person was married, gather some information about how the couple met each other, how many children they had, and how long they were married. If step- children were involved, you will want to know them as well. Having the names of the children can give your eulogy more of a personal touch to it and make the family feel more together again.

Be involved as you are asking questions. Make positive comments to their responses, so that your interview does not appear as an interrogation. Keep in mind; some families are going to be much more open to share than others will be. Sometimes the people you are interviewing will be learning things for the first time from each other as questions are being answered.

- When and where did you meet?
- Who was the first one to take interest in the other?
- How did your proposal take place?
- What trait did you admire the most in your spouse?
- Who was the disciplinarian with the kids?
- What were the kids' names?
- How did you divide up your roles as husband and wife?
- What trait did your spouse admire the most in you?
- What will you miss the most with your spouse not being here?

You will want to get some information on the person's religious background so that what you say in the eulogy conforms to what the person actually professed or believed. You can be honest in your eulogy without being judgmental. There are some universal truths about all people when it comes to God. All people are created by God. God fashions everyone in his or her mother's womb. God has a plan and a purpose for every life. Everyone's life is a gift from God. God desires to be in a relationship with everyone. God blesses everyone with certain skills and talents whether they acknowledge God or not. Everyone will die and go back to God. If the person is a believer, you will want to know the following information.

- When did the person acknowledge God in his/her life?
- What church/religious institution did the person attend?
- What positions or services did the person do in the life of the church/religious institution?
- What part of the church/religious institution did the person enjoy the most?

You should conclude the interview process with an emphasis on the person. Some of the responses you get will have already been given in some of the previous questions. This will be a chance for some people to think of some things they had not thought of before. It also ends the interview process on a positive note.

- What were some specific sayings that this person was known for saying?
- What were some specific mannerisms this person had that you expected to see?
- What would this person have really wanted to be known for?
- What would have made this person truly happy before he/she died?

One of the blessings from doing the interview with a group of family members is that the process itself brings a sense of healing to those who participate. Just sharing positive things about the deceased person builds a bond within the group. It also builds a trust level between you and the group. You will have to use wisdom in knowing which of the stories that have been shared with you, should remain private, and which ones can help you in your eulogy. You should conclude the interviewing process by thanking everyone for their participation and letting them know they have helped you tremendously, even though you won't be able to use everything they have shared. Offer to pray for the family and for the upcoming service.

The Gathering & Sorting Process

Before you start, ask God for wisdom on how to be most effective in ministering to the audience that will be present for the service. Once you have gathered your information together you need to read through the information and see if you can pick up a common thread that seems to have run throughout the person's life. For instance did a dominant feature of the person's life revolve around generosity, protecting others, courage, fighting injustice, forgiveness, acceptance, hard - working, commitment to God, servant's heart, Good Samaritan, dependability, reliability, or caring for others?

Once you identify the theme, you will want to bring it up throughout your eulogy. This will help those who knew the person to feel more connected to what you are saying. If the person is a believer, finding a bible verse that highlights that particular theme and using it early in your message will also draw more people into what you are saying.

One advantage of discovering the dominant theme is, you will be enabled to eliminate some of the information that was presented to you by the group. Not every good story can be woven into your eulogy. Some of the stories will take you off on a tangent, and some of them are too personal or private to be repeated. You do not want to share something in your eulogy that may be hurtful to someone else who is present. For instance in some families, they may joke about one kid being the favorite and how the kids used it to their advantage. In other families, someone may tell a story about someone being the favorite, but you can tell there is hostility and resentment behind the statement. You do not want to mention anything about favorites in your eulogy. Be sensitive in how much you may praise one family member and neglect another. You will also want to be sensitive as to how you are to mention prior spouses especially in the case of divorces.

I was doing a eulogy once for a pastor whose wife had died, and he had remarried. His daughter, who was present, was from the first marriage along with his second wife. I handled the situation by saying "He was blessed to be married to two wonderful wives. But don't get too excited, he was only married to one of them at a time." I was then able to speak briefly about the first marriage and then go on to tell how much he loved and appreciated his second wife."

You will have several options available to you on organizing your information into a story format. Everything does not have to necessary flow in chronological order. Sometimes the information you have to work with will only cover a short period of a person's life. You work with what you have. You can put your eulogy together in several different ways depending on the story you want to tell.

A good story is going to have several different kinds of emotions involved. The same should be true of your eulogy. You want the people to learn something new about the person, you want them to laugh together, you want them to feel sadness together, and you want them thankful they were there to hear the eulogy. A good eulogy leaves people on an upbeat note when you are done. Build some suspense in your stories. Don't just give out facts.

Organize your information in an outline form so that you can pull it all together in your eulogy. My outline will often look like this:

- Introduction
- One Word Names
- Childhood Information
- Birth Family Information
- Marriage –Wedding Story
- Kids Information
- Community Service

- Marriage-Family
- Religious Background
- Message On Heaven

If the person is a believer, you will want to weave the hand of God from beginning to end in the message so that the person's life is not cut up into independent spheres. You want to use humor in your message as much as appropriate, but the humor has to come out of the person's life and not from a joke or a story that you're tempted to tell because it's funny.

You can take negative traits of a person, and use humor to mention the trait so that everyone knows you are being real in your message. For instance, if it is obvious that the person was very bossy of others, you may say something such as "Even though some of you may have thought Bob was very bossy, he actually was a strong leader determined to take a specific course of action." If someone was a tightwad with money, you can say something such as "many of you know that Sue was saving whatever money she could get for that rainy day. Unfortunately if you needed some of it before the rainy day arrived, you were not going to get it.

If your tradition allows for family members to give testimonies during the service, some of the family members will tell some of the same stories at the service that they told you in the interview. You need to listen so that you know how to handle it, if you have that same story written in your message. Sometimes it may be appropriate to not mention it in your message, but other times you may want to keep the story in your message and expand upon it. Listen to the testimonies that are given during the service, and you will have additional material for your message especially if you did not get very much information during the interview process.

Before I actually begin my eulogy, I ask everyone to stand so that we might remember ____________ publicly one last time, and I pray for the audience and that God will use the eulogy to help us be drawn closer to him. I do this for practical reasons. First we need God's blessings and second we may need a stand up break. Some people will have been seated for a long time depending on the length of the service, and it is good to give them an opportunity to stretch. It also makes everyone more receptive to hearing your eulogy.

In your introduction, provide the background of what was taking place in the world or nation at the time of the person's birth. You can do it this very easily by typing in "events and the date of the person's birth" in google. Choose a couple of interesting events from this time period and tell them as a story beginning with the date. Then contrast those events with a "but in the hills of West Virginia, in the city of Blue Fish, God was sending a gift into the world through Mary and John Smith in the form of a little that we all know as Carry." Starting your message as a story teller engages people into your message. The better story teller you are, the more people will remember the eulogy and the greater impact that it will have.

If you did not know the person for whom you are doing the eulogy, you should come out and say something such us, “I didn’t know Carry personally, but I can tell you what she was like from the testimonies of her family and friends. When I asked them from some one word descriptions of Carry, I was given words such as:” (Here you would use the words you got in your interview when you asked for one word descriptions.) You want to say each word with force and a tone that describes the word itself. You do not want to simply read them as a list. Remember, you are telling a story in your eulogy. Be authentic with your message.

The Writing--The Anatomy Of A Eulogy

The following is an anatomy of a eulogy that was done for a Christian husband and father who died unexpectedly of a heart attack while delivering newspapers on a Sunday morning. I had expected to interview several members of his family, but the only persons present for the interview were his wife and two sons. I had spoken with his sister two days before the interview when my wife and I had visited the family the initial day he died. I will attempt to explain the process as the eulogy was being written to help you understand why it is being constructed in the manner that it is. With time, you will develop your own thought processes.

One of the things I learned about Douglas during the interview was that he was a person who loved trivia, and the overall theme of his life was standing up for justice. So I began the message with those two things in mind for my introduction.

I choose events that had to do with fights for justice and the kind of trivia that Douglas would answer from jeopardy. I also wanted to weave God's story into Douglas' life from the very beginning since he was a believer.

Eulogy For Douglas Thomas

In May of 1943, the world was at war and freedom and justice was at stake. In Poland, the Germans had crushed the last of the Resistance in the Warsaw Ghetto Uprising killing thousands of Jews and sending the rest to the Treblinka concentration camp to die.

Meanwhile in Alaska, American troops were battling Japanese soldiers on the island of Attu in the Aleutian Islands to retake the Island from the Japanese troops.

But God was busy raising up a one man army that would be fighting for a different kind of freedom and justice by sending into the world a little black boy in Welch, West

Virginia who would pass through this life being called Douglas Thomas.

You see when God created Douglas; he was creating a one of a kind. The Scriptures tell us Psalm 139:13-16 For you created my inmost being; you knit me together in my mother's womb. 14I praise you because I am fearfully and wonderfully made; your works are wonderful, I know that full well. 15My frame was not hidden from you when I was made in the secret place. When I was woven together in the depths of the earth, 6your eyes saw my unformed body. All the days ordained for me were written in your book before one of them came to be.

You can use the Scriptures from Psalm 139 above for any person whether they knew the Lord or not because it is still true of them. In the next section of the message, I used some of the one word descriptions that I had been given by the family to insert them into the message. Some of the words I had been given were patient, humble, humorous, thoughtful, passionate, justice, full of wisdom, and determined.

I used the words in story format hence I wrote a story of God thinking about creating Douglas. I want to keep Doug and God tied throughout the eulogy to keep the interest of all the people in the service wherever they are spiritually. The goal of a eulogy for a believer is to use the person's life story to point others to Christ.

> In other words, none of us just happened. We came into this world, having been put together by God to make a difference in the lives of others and to make a difference for God. It's amazing the different ingredients God uses to put us together in our mother's womb.

> God must have been thinking, this fellow Doug is going to be a tough one in order to accomplish what I'm calling him to do. I've got to put enough fire and passion in his bones to demand justice and freedom, wherever he finds oppression and chains, but I've got to give him enough wisdom to know when to speak and when to wait.

I've got to give him enough humor not only to make him able to bring laughter in the lives of others, but to use it to get past his own pain and humiliation that he will experience in his journey of life.

I've got to make him curious enough to want to fill his mind with all kinds of facts and trivia but humble enough not to show off. I've got to make him patient enough to pass on the wisdom I will give to him to those who will not want to listen.

I've got to make him strong enough to be a great protector, yet gentle enough to be thoughtful of others in just the right moment. I've got to make him the kind of leader who knows how to walk alone when needed, but who is at his best in his hands on service to others.

I'll give him just enough stubbornness to keep others from walking over him. That should about do it. I'll leave a touch of my spirit, that He might know he came from me and one day he's to come back to me. Get ready world, here comes one of my special gifts to you.

The goal of the next part of the eulogy is an attempt to challenge the audience to see themselves from God's perspective. I also wanted to bring in current events as they related to Douglas' life. Douglas was an African American and his funeral was being held during Black History month. When you are writing a eulogy, see what impact the person's life is having in today's world. God places us in a specific period of time for a specific purpose. We are called to serve God in our generation, not some other.

> We are all a gift from God to the rest of the world. Life is the process of opening that gift and using that gift to enrich the lives of others. Unfortunately, far too many of us think, that the gift is to be an end in and of itself. All efforts are directed back on the gift itself.
>
> Douglas Thomas was a man who understood that life is not found in seeking to simply please one's self. The more lives

you touch, the more enjoyable life becomes. In a day and a time, when a good man may be hard to find, I want you to know there are still some good men and that Douglas Thomas was one of them.

I believe one of the greatest celebrations of Black History Month is taking place right here, right now in the Celebration of An African American Man who knew the true meaning of being there for his family, actively participated in his Church, and stood up for those who could not speak up for themselves.

I wanted people to know the early historical situation that helped to shape Doug's life, but I inserted humor in it to keep serious topics like racism and prejudice somewhat light. Using irony such as "the huge city of Wells, West, VA" helped people to laugh and to forget the sadness of the occasion. Putting things in story form keeps your audience engaged with you, so know the stories well that you are going to tell in your eulogy. Once again I wanted to hit on the theme of social justice but using it with humor to show people a side of Doug they had not known before.

> Doug didn't start out on the top of society. If you are Black, the third of 8 children, born in the 40's, in a huge city like Wells, W. VA you better believe you were going to know something about poverty, about suffering, and about racism. Even moving to a larger city like Wellsville, OH was not going to change that.
>
> Doug's first encounter with trying to overcome the injustice of racism happened as a young boy. This little Caucasian kid would seek to humiliate Doug in a crowd by calling him a nigger as loud as he could. He did this several times in public. But Doug was a patient little fellow and did not take matters into his hand.
>
> One day however Doug and his brother came across this kid and he was by himself. Even though Dr. King was getting his

movement going in Montgomery with the bus strike, Doug at this point had not fully understood the doctrine of non-violence so he attempted to make a change in this young man's behavior by giving him a beating. Doug then turned the young fellow over to his brother to further administer justice against prejudice and bigotry. Although Doug's methods were unorthodox, that young man ceased to use the N word again in Doug's presence.

Doug did enter into a period in which he sought to undo classism and economic inequality at an early age. Doug thoroughly understood the principle that God causes all things to grow. It appears that God was causing too many watermelons to grow in other people's fields and there were times when Doug attempted to bring about a socialist revolution by redistributing the watermelons under the cloak of darkness to his friends and family without informing the owner of the watermelons.

There were times when the owner made attempts to talk to Doug about this matter, but Doug was never available for a discussion since he was fleeing the scene of the crime, I mean economic exploitation.

Doug went on in life to study the law so that he could deal with situations like this in a more appropriate manner.

During the interview process, I was given very little information on Doug's work history but I received quite a bit of information on his family life. That was going to be the center thrust of the message because family meant so much to Doug. Even with the family you can still see Doug's quality of social justice at work in him in the respect that he had for his wife and kids. I chose to tell the story of his courtship with his wife because she was so proud of it during the interview process. It also was a chance to build a story with a surprise in it. Nobody would have thought Ella would have turned Doug down with his first proposal of marriage. When you are interviewing the family, listen for those moments that can be turned into a good story with a surprise ending.

Doug and Ella had a very good marriage, and I wanted to show the audience what made them the happy couple that they were. All of the information came from doing the interview questions. I also wanted to lift up Doug's treatment of his wife as a role model for other men to follow and as an indication that Christ was at work in Doug in his home.

> Doug always had a keen insight into knowing when he had discovered something good. He had met this young college student, when he was a graduate student in North Carolina. Doug went on to Cleveland to accept a job there. Years later this beautiful young college student had also moved to Cleveland to accept a job. Now Doug began to put operation "Doug the man" into action.
>
> He asked this young lady by the name of Ella on a date. She accepted it. She remembered that he was one of the kindest and most thoughtful guys she had ever met. He treated her with the utmost of respect. One day Doug got up the courage to ask her to marry him. She was a 23 year old beauty at the time. If you had of seen her, you would have known why Doug wanted her so

badly. Doug waited with great anticipation for her answer.

Her response was," No, I'm not ready for marriage yet." Now most people would have heard rejection, but Doug chose to hear the word "yet." So his response was, "the next time I ask you, you will be ready." He continued to lay on the charm and the sweetness. His family fell in love with her and she with them.

As the years starting ticking past, Ella was starting to get a little nervous. She now realized this one, was a good one and she was hoping he might ask her again soon. Doug managed to wait three years before coming out to ask the question again. Just like he had prophesied three years earlier, this time she was going to be ready to say yes, and yes it was. They took a journey together that lasted 44 years and brought countless moments of joy, laughter and tears with each other. They knew what it was to be best friends together and to truly share life together.

There is a verse in the bible directed at husbands. It is a simple one, but not often carried out. It is "husbands love your wives as Christ loved the church and gave himself up for her." Doug humbled himself so that he could love his wife as Christ loved the church.

Ella speaks of the mutual respect they had for each other. Doug was eager to support her in her dreams and in her career. He realized God had a calling on each of their lives, and that true love required that hey help each other to become all that God intended for each of them to be.

Men, we could take a few cues from Doug. His love was proactive when it came to their sons. He would tell Ella, "you go out and do something for yourself, I've got the kids. He told her, "You have no business going to the gas station." So he saw to it that her car stayed full of gas. He told her, "My wife cannot be seen in a dirty car." So he kept it clean. Ella sat beck and soaked it all in.

They had a kitchen partnership. She would cook and he would do the dishes. If she tried to put the dishes in the dishwasher, he would take them back out so that they could be put in the right way. Ella experienced what it was like to be loved by Douglas Thomas and I think her testimony to him was the same as James Taylor when he sang "How sweet it is to be loved by you."

Douglas had two sons and both of them had participated in the interview process and given me information about their father. They were the only two on the program who were going to give testimonies during the service. I had wanted to tell a story about each of the boys with their fathers, but I had no way of knowing in advance, what stories either son would tell about their father at the service. Fortunately, Jason did not mention anything that I had in the eulogy about him and his father. Cedric spoke after Jason and Cedric did mention his father being their when he broke the school long jump record.

What I did when I got to that part of the eulogy in the actual service was to say that Cedric had been too humble just like his father in telling about how he broke the school record. I then retold the story of him warming up, running down the lane, soaring into the air, coming down further than anyone before him and shattering the 80 year old record. I retold it, rather than deleting it, because the point I wanted to make was that it was God's gift to them both, that his father was present the day the record was broken. I also wanted to weave in Doug's belief in the word of God so that when I did truly speak of God in the end, people would not think I had made a dramatic shift in the message. You will also see the social justice theme pop up again, this time in relationship to his son Jason.

> Doug saw their sons, Cedric and Jason as much as his responsibility as they were his wife. He felt insulted if someone asked him if he was babysitting his kids. He'd let them know that he wasn't babysitting, he was being their father.
>
> He was determined to follow the biblical command given to fathers, which was Fathers do not provoke your children, but bring them up in the training and instruction

of the Lord. Both of his sons appreciated their father's spiritual discipline and the patience he demonstrated to them in explaining what was right and what was wrong.

Doug wanted his children to know that he loved them and that he would be there for them no matter what the circumstances. He taught them to have a "never give up attitude" no matter how difficult things might become. But his sons remember the fun loving comical dad that they had, who always had their back. Both sons were athletes, and they would go to a game or meet in some small town, they had never heard of and their dad would show up to cheer them on. He took every opportunity to use it to help them grow into men.

Jason said his school was so small, they had to have girls on their team. When Jason went off the court or came on the court, he would give the guys a high five but he ignored the girls. His father picked up on this and after the game explained to him, "you must show the girls the same respect and encouragement that you give to the guys on the team." That teachable moment instilled the idea of justice and equality into Jason.

Sometimes I think that God orchestrates special moments in our lives so that they can be shared together. Cedric was having a track meet. This particular day, Doug left work to be there. Cedric was a long jumper. He came running down the pathway, took a leap up into the air, and when he landed on the other side he had broken an 80 year old school record.

It was a joy for him to share that moment with his dad. Cedric wanted to know, how his dad knew to be there that day. His father told him, he just had a feeling today would be the day. I think it was God giving them a special son and dad moment together.

Now there were a couple of things that Doug did as a father that probably were not the best of examples but it sure gave his son something to remember. They were at home and it was hot afternoon. They had no air conditioning. Doug did remember there was air conditioning at the movie theater.

So he asked Jason if he would like to go to the movies. They went, but not before Doug grabbed his heavy winter coat. You see they had not eaten yet. They had a bucket of chicken. Jason remembers it being about 90 degrees and his father walking into the theater in this heavy winter coat in order to hide a bucket of chicken underneath. They smuggled the chicken into the theatre and had a nice cool afternoon.

The same love that Doug had for his kids, he had for his grandkids. He wanted Cedric to be an even better father than he had been, and so he would send Cedric books on how to parent and how to be a good father.

A eulogy should seek to touch as many people there as possible to make them feel included. I knew that Doug's sisters and brothers would be there, but I didn't have stories from them. I did have his sister's comments about the sacrifices he had made for them. The purpose of this paragraph was to let Doug's brothers and sisters know that they had not been forgotten. A good eulogy is going to lift the spirits of as many people possible at the service. Be over generous with your recognition of others. Include others in your overall theme of the person's life whenever possible.

> Doug's generosity moved beyond his immediate family. His sister said of her younger brother," he was always trying to be the big brother for us all." At the heart of Doug was his love for the times when his family got together. He and Ella each came from families with 8 children, so there was always plenty of family to go around. Doug did not mind investing himself into the lives of others.

In the next paragraph I want people to clearly understand that Douglas was involved in the life of the church, and that it was the call of Christ that shaped and influenced his life. I mention both he and his wife in their generosity because they always made their contributions as a couple. That kind of partnership deserves recognition. As one of Doug's pastors, I shared my experiences with Doug, and again I bring in the theme of Doug's life on the issue of social justice. I will also attempt to transition the focus from Doug to the gospel itself.

> Doug and Ella were always generous in their support of the special outreaches of the church. If you look at the special projects done by Glenville in the lobby area of our church, you're going to find their names. Doug was one of the charter covenant partners here at New Life At Calvary. When we first began our merger talks to create New Life At Calvary, Doug was there with thoughtful questions for the group to consider.
>
> Doug would often leave you a word of encouragement with your sermon on his way out the door. If you preached a sermon involving social justice or overcoming oppression, Doug was going to let you know that was a really good message. Doug walked through life with a quiet and humble spirit.
>
> He wasn't out front leading the masses, but he was one who came alongside of you,

changing lives one life at a time. He had a couple of saying, “First Things First” in other words stay focused and the other one was , “There is only one February 5th, 2016 make the most of it.” Each day is a gift, so treat it as such.

What made the difference in Douglas Thomas that set him apart from so many fathers, so many husbands, and so many men today? It’s simple. He had enough vision to make his life count in the service of others. One day he heard a voice that called him to die. I’m not talking about the death he had Sunday, but one that he heard a while back that said, if anyone wants to become my disciple, he must pick up his cross, deny himself and come follow me. Doug heard the call of Jesus Christ. He made a decision to give his life to follow after Jesus Christ. It was a decision of his heart and of his mind.

If a person died and did not know Christ or you are unaware of the person’s relationship to God, you can still transition to a gospel message without being judgmental about the person. Keep in mind, we never know what a person may have said to God within their final moments of life. You can say something to the effect, “We can be thankful for the gift that Carry was to us. Just as God sent Carry into the world, God has called Carry back to Himself, as God will one day call each of us. Are you aware of what the Bible teaches about the afterlife?” At that point, you can share the gospel message with the people.

Since Doug knew the Lord, in the paragraphs below, I wanted to share the gospel as though Doug himself was attempting to share it. Since I have been bringing in references to God throughout the message, the transition from Doug to God is a much smoother one. I want to give a brief presentation of the gospel and conclude the presentation by bringing Doug back into the picture so that the audience will know, Doug took the step himself, and it made a difference in his life.

Douglas Thomas has left behind a legacy of ordained days and has gone home to be with Jesus Christ. You may think, with all the joy and laughter he brought into the lives of his family and friends, and with all the love and commitment he gave to his wife, children, and grandchildren, that Doug certainly deserves to go to heaven.

But if could speak to us today, he would say that's not quite true. You see, according to the Bible, none of us deserves to go to heaven. Did you know that according to Jesus, most people will not go to heaven?

Jesus said in , Mat 7:13 "Enter through the narrow gate. For wide is the gate and broad is the road that leads to destruction, and many enter through it. But small is the gate and narrow the road that leads to life, and only a few find it. We were all on that road to destruction. We have to choose to get out of it.

You see we find in **John 3:16-18 (NIV)**
[16] "For God so loved the world that he gave his one and only Son, that whoever believes in him shall not perish but have eternal life.
[17] For God did not send his Son into the world to condemn the world, but to save the

world through him. [18] Whoever believes in him is not condemned, but whoever does not believe stands condemned already because he has not believed in the name of God's one and only Son.

Entering into a personal relationship with Jesus Christ is the only way to enter that narrow gate. All you have to do is to admit, "God, I have done a lot of things I should not have done. I realize I cannot pay for all that I have done. I ask you for forgiveness. I accept that when Jesus Christ died on the cross, He being holy and righteous, paid the penalty for my sin. I invite him to come into my life and take control of it." Douglas made that decision years ago and has not regretted it since.

You will make numerous decisions in your life between your birth and your death. But the only decision that will still be personally affecting you a 1000 years from today, is what did you do with Jesus Christ. The Bible teaches there will certainly be a resurrection of everybody from the dead, and then comes the judgment of God. That judgement involves a reality of heaven and hell. God raised Jesus from the dead to let us

> know there is an afterlife and we shall spend eternity in one place or another.
>
> Douglas Thomas is prepared for that Judgment. Like the Apostle Paul he can say, and the time has come for my departure. I have fought the good fight, I have finished the race, I have kept the faith. Now there is in store for me the crown of righteousness, which the Lord, the righteous Judge, will award to me on that day--and not only to me, but also to all who have longed for his appearing.

In the paragraph below I want to finally conclude the message by connecting everyone there back to Douglas in some form of relationship and offer them a promise and a hope as to why this is not the end. God is making a reunion possible for all of us present if we desire to make it so. I end the message quoting 1 Thessalonians 4:13-18 because it speaks of the resurrection in a very positive and uplifting way. This ends the eulogy on a positive note, and it allows the word of God to speak for itself. You should read the passage with feeling and emotion, building up to a crescendo at the very end.

We may say of Douglas Thomas , that he was my friend, he was my uncle, he was my brother, he was my father, or he was my husband, but the greatest truth of them all is that Douglas Thomas is and forever will be a child of God who has now completely returned to God. For those of us who die without knowing Jesus Christ. Douglas Thomas will only be a memory, a very good and loving memory. But for those of us who do know Jesus Christ, Douglas Thomas . is simply waiting to meet us on the other side.

For the Bible clearly teaches, in 1 Th 4:13 Brothers and sisters , we do not want you to be ignorant about those who fall asleep, or to grieve like the rest of men and women, who have no hope. We believe that Jesus died and rose again and so we believe that God will bring with Jesus those who have fallen asleep in him. According to the Lord's own word, we tell you that we who are still alive, who are left till the coming of the Lord, will certainly not precede those who have fallen asleep.

> For the Lord himself will come down from heaven, with a loud command, with the voice of the archangel and with the trumpet call of God, and the dead in Christ will rise first. After that, we who are still alive and are left will be caught up together with them in the clouds to meet the Lord in the air. And so we will be with the Lord forever.

Once you have written your eulogy, the next step is to preach it and record it. Listen to your message more than once and you will get a feel for what flows in the message and what does not. The better you know your eulogy, the less dependent on the paper you will be, and the better your delivery will come across. Be aware of how long your eulogy is. It will probably be five to 10 minutes longer during the service than it is when you preach it to yourself. Be attuned to your audience and they will let you know if you should start to wrap up things sooner than you had expected. Remember again, you do not have to tell everything the person has done in life.

Writing An Obituary

Many things that are written in the Obituary do not have to be reemphasized in your eulogy, especially if there is a reading of the obituary. If the family needs help writing the obituary, the interview questions can provide them with guidelines for the information that is needed. If your assistance is needed in writing the obituary think in terms of paragraph. The first paragraph lists the date and place of birth, the parents' name, the number of brothers and sisters, and something about where the person grew up. The second paragraph lists the person's educational background, work history, hobbies and community activities. The third paragraph lists the person's marriage and immediate family background, and interesting facts about the person.

The fourth paragraph lists the persons civic groups, religious affiliations and service. The paragraph may conclude with the death of the person. The final paragraph lists the names of the people who have survived the deceased person. Some families will want to include all family members even those who are deceased. There is no right or wrong answer to this, so include whomever the family wants to include in the obituary. Also the arrangement of the information in the paragraphs above is subject to what the family prefers. I have just offered some guidelines. You may have more paragraphs depending on the person's accomplishments and how much space you have available.

Additional Eulogy Resources.

If you would like to see various introductions for eulogies, you can look at the numerous eulogies I have written on the website sermoncentral.com. All you have to do is go to the site, search for funerals in tag box, and choose the category Presbyterian/Reformed in the Denomination box. A myriad of sermons concerning funerals will come up on the listing. Just look for the sermons under Rick Gillespie-Mobley.

Having been in ministry for nearly 34 years, I have done funerals for just about every kind of a circumstance. There are eulogies on the sermoncentral.com site by me for people who were at various places on the spiritual spectrum from non-believers to the most committed of believers. There are eulogies for people who were murdered, who committed suicide, who died suddenly and unexpected, and people who lived to be 105. There are eulogies for people of all ages. There are eulogies for people I loved dearly both from my own family and from the life of the church. A good eulogy can be a powerful source of strength and closure for a family. It will point people in the direction of Jesus Christ.

If you would like to see me actually preach this sermon of which I have done an anatomy for in the book you can go to https://vimeo.com/156871145. You will get much more of a story telling feel than you can get from simply reading the sermon. Thank you for your purchase of this e-book. I hope you will tell others about the book as well. Do feel free to contact me if you have any questions.

Acknowledgment By The Author

Thank you for taking the time to purchase this book. The goal of this book is to help you produce quality eulogies which will be a blessing to those who are left behind. You will will help to remember the deceased in a manner that will be worthy of their lives.

Sincerely

Rick Gillespie-Mobley

rickntoby@gnlcc.com

New Life At Calvary

2020 East 79th Street

Cleveland, OH .44103

newlifeatcalvar.org

attorneyrgm@gnlcc.com

Other Books By The Author

The Screwtape Orders

Is God In The Crisis

20 Small Group Bible Studies

Growing In Christ Through The Book Of James: 12 Bible Studies

The Art Of Becoming Great Ushers & Greeters

Black History Sermons

Easter Holy Week Sermons

Father's Day Or Men's Day Sermons

Mother Day Sermons